2

How to Train Your Human:

A Guide for Parrots

4

Sandy Lender and Petri Lender

How to Train Your Human:
A Guide for Parrots

*A primer on caring for pet birds,
told by an awesome companion parrot
from the bulge in his bird cozy*

Sandy Lender Ink Inc./Florida

Sandy Lender Ink Inc.
Florida
USA

Copyright © Sandy Lender, 2019
All rights reserved. No part of this book may be reproduced, scanned, or distributed in any printed or electronic form without permission. Please do not participate in or encourage piracy of copyrighted materials in violation of the author's rights.
Purchase only authorized editions.

Neither Sandy Lender Ink Inc. nor any of its agents is responsible for any harm that comes from the use or misuse of this book or the contents herein. Consult your avian veterinarian, not an online group, with your questions regarding pet bird health.

Originally published in the United States of America.

ISBN 978-0-999-8780-3-3

Printed in the United States of America

Book design by Sandy Lender

*Dedicated to all the parrots
who are still training their humans
to do things right.*

Contents

Acknowledgments 11

Foreword, by Tony Silva 13

1] Choose a Human You Can Train Easily 17
    How I Chose My Human
    Your Cuteness Matters as Much as Your Intelligence

2] The Story of the Egg 21

3] How to Train Your Human 25
    Selecting Your Favorite Song
    Requesting a Bath Bowl (with a clean-air discussion)
    Bird-Safe Produce Wash
    Bird-Safe Upholstery Cleaner
    Bird-Safe Glass Cleaner
    Eyeglasses: Perching vs. Tugging
    Why Fly When You Can Ride?

4] Shirt Surfing and Other Extreme Contact Sports 37

5] Sometimes Humans are Difficult to Understand 43
    How to Protect Yourself from Poisonous Foods
    Other Evils in the Tree

6] Relaxing in Safe Trees 47
    Your Tree
    How to Evacuate with Minimal Stress

7] Some Birds Live Through Scary Stuff...............................51
   Teka and Ernie's Story
   Bobo's Story
   Bobo's List of Grievances

8] Everybirdie Needs a Medical File..57
   The Orange Folder
   The Fragile Eclectus

9] Sometimes Ya Gotta Pluck..67

10] Your Human Will Cook for You 71
    Chopped Veggie Mashup Explained
    Special Recipes from Petri's Kitchen

Epilogue..81

Acknowledgments

Petri would like to thank Brenda, wherever she is today.

Sandy would like to thank Petri, who helped her understand the concept of loving someone unconditionally.

To friends like Jennine, Marci, Maryann, and Wendy, who have performed bird-sitting duties over the years, you don't know the level of trust Sandy placed in you letting you safeguard the darling—and demanding—Petri the Great. Thank you to Dr. Andazola at Cape Coral Veterinary Clinic, who didn't laugh at Sandy when she introduced Petri, saying, "This is the flock leader."

Thank you to Tony Silva who took the time to read the unformatted manuscript and write the foreword. Thank you to the professionals at Top Shelf Editing for content and line editing advice.

Thank you to every aviculturist and bird enthusiast who has shared kind and well-intentioned advice for the betterment of companion parrot ownership. We're all in this together to make sure our pet birds are as healthy and happy as possible.

Foreword

It was a cool day when I travelled north from Miami to a much-awaited resurrection of the Organization of Professional Aviculturists meeting in Tampa. This organization was formed to represent bird breeders and owners at a state level to ensure that our voices would be heard. Present at that meeting was Sandy Lender. We spoke briefly, but during that conversation one fact emerged clearly: her passion for parrots.

We met again about a year later. This time there were birds around us. I watched her as she would talk to, gently caress, and handle birds. Her contact with them was clearly based on experience. She was not just a person casually interested in parrots, but rather was an individual who understood the complex, unpredictable, and demanding personalities of parrots.

When Sandy first discussed with me this book, I smiled. She could bring a fresh perspective to bird keeping, using as her basis her passion and understanding of this most incredible group of birds. Sandy was also proposing to write the book from a bird's perspective. This unique view was through the eyes of Petri, her sun conure (*Aratinga solstitialis*). No one had ever written a book on parrots as *they* see *us*. I was thus extremely curious as to what the final product would look like.

When the manuscript arrived, I took it with me on a trip to study wild parrots in Argentina. I would have time in the evening to focus on the manuscript and not have the typical household distractions of a busy home.

My first step was to quickly peruse the book. If that glance would not spark my interest, I would decline the invitation to write this foreword. But as I roamed quickly past the pages, I found myself absorbed. I could not quickly glance at sentences, but rather I stopped to read sections.

At some point I halted this exercise and started reading from the beginning. I found the book witty, interesting, and a great venue to convey good information. Here was a book of how parrots see us. It described their needs and their manner. I could see why Sandy had won Best Literary Fiction Novel Award in 2019 because of her concise manner, but I could also see experience seeping across every word. She was talking from experience. This was not someone reading several articles on the Internet and writing a book. This was years of experience being put on paper.

Petri the sun conure uses the book as a platform to teach pet owners, aviculturists, and experienced breeders. His perspective will allow the owner of one or many parrots of any species to better understand this large group of birds. This understanding is vital because many parrot owners make mistakes, which results in the birds not being properly maintained, in plucking, in incessant screaming, or in the bird being regarded as expendable and relinquished.

My view after reading the book and absorbing every word is that it will permit better bird ownership. As a seasoned aviculturist, field researcher and breeder, I took away a new perspective. I believe you, the reader, will feel the same.

To Sandy, I state kudos, and to Petri, my congratulations, because he has managed to teach us all about proper bird ownership. To the reader, my fervent hope is that this book will teach you about the demanding and rewarding experience of having a parrot as part of your family.

—Tony Silva, Author of *Psittaculture*
Former Curator of Loro Parque, Tenerife

How to Train Your Human:
A Guide for Parrots

Chapter 1
Choose a Human You Can Train Easily
How I Chose My Human
My human named me after the young pterodactyl in the 1988 movie *The Land Before Time*. I've not watched that cartoon, but my research leads me to understand pterodactyls were immense predators with razor-sharp talons, keen eyesight, and ferocious beaks of death. I like that. Sandy chose well when selecting the name Petri for me.

I chose well when selecting her as my human.

I hatched with four other eggs. My bird mother and bird father were exceptionally beautiful with feathers colored deep orange like fire and vivid yellow like the sun. My siblings were adequately cute. Brenda, the first human in my life, worked night and day to make sure we five chicks had all the comforts we needed in our nest box. I would learn later that she had the title "breeder."

Some people say that title with derision. Sandy and I know Brenda was an awesome lady, so we don't snarl when we reminisce about her. We smile. We're both thankful that Brenda brought us together. Here's how that happened.

Nineteen full years ago, I hatched alongside four brothers and sisters. We lived with Brenda and her family, at first. Her family was kind, but my bird parents informed me she'd be moving far away, and all five chicks had to be sold to new homes beforehand.

One night, Sandy and her husband came to visit us. One of my sisters had already gone to live at her new home, so I understood the drill. When Sandy came in, I knew she was the lady I wanted to live with. She seemed like the kind of lady who would cave to my every whim.

The four of us chicks climbed around on Sandy while she sat on the floor, and we pretended she was a tree in the Amazon rain forest. It was great. She laughed a lot, which I thought was a good sign, and she didn't mind at all that we weren't potty-trained.

I stayed close to her the whole time she sat talking to Brenda, but toward the end of her visit, the humans placed all four of us in front of our cage. I feared Sandy was going to leave without me! My heart rate quickened as alarm bells sounded in my birdie brain. I'd never find another human as easy to train as Sandy, and I knew it.

As soon as Brenda let go of me, I waddled back to Sandy as fast as I could, shaking my tail feathers behind me. I made it back to her before any of my dawdling siblings, and climbed up the front of her blue shirt. It seemed appropriate to poop on her shoulder to mark her as mine.

The other three chicks toddled over, as well, but they were slow. Sandy said that meant I was supposed to be her forever bird.

She was right.

Brenda wrote down the numbers on my leg band for her records before I went home with Sandy. Brenda had secured the band above my foot before I even had feathers. It's kinda fancy, and I'm so used to it, I hardly realize it's there most of the time. Sandy says it's important because it can help identify me if anything horrifying should ever happen. I don't know what horrifying things could happen, but I trust her judgment on this.

You see, another bird in our flock doesn't have his leg band, and Sandy went through all kinds of troubles trying to locate health records for him. She was never able to find those documents, so we had to start over with his health history. It was a little scary, but we can talk about that later. Right now, we're talking about how I got my human mom.

Once we got to our first tree, which we would share, I had to start training Sandy, of course. Even if a human has lived with a bird in her past, she will require re-conditioning to be truly ready to care for a sun conure *(Aratinga solstitialis)* or other parrot of such magnificence.

I'm fortunate that Sandy has always been willing to learn. This book may be oversimplified for some parrots because my human was easy to train. If you find that your human is difficult to work with, some of the subtler ideas in this book may not work for you. I've met humans who needed to be hit over the head with a Manzanita branch to get their attention; Sandy and I lived with one like that for a while. We'll take a look at some ways to get those humans to behave properly. May this book serve as a guide for your most relaxed and happiest avian life.

Let's start with some resources Sandy recommends online:
- www.aav.org/page/basiccare;
- www.proaviculture.com/articles.htm;
- sandy-lender-ink.teachable.com/p/how-to-care-for-your-bird;
- www.ziggyshaven.com;
- birdgardensofnaples.org;
- birdvet.com.au/;
- brookfallsveterinary.com/; and
- vcahospitals.com/know-your-pet/plants-safe-for-birds.

Sandy says, when you look for veterinary information or sites online, don't let that be a substitute for a real-life veterinarian's guidance. If one of us is showing signs of illness, owners should put down the computer/tablet and take us to the vet with questions. Don't wait.

Your Cuteness Matters
As Much as Your Intelligence
We parrots are incredibly smart. One parrot famous for proving our intelligence was Alex the African grey parrot *(Psittacus erithacus)*, whom you can find information about on the site https://alexfoundation.org/. The research foundation Dr. Irene Pepperberg formed out of his greatness still carries on its work today, proving the amazing capacity for learning—and teaching—that we cool birds possess.

What the stories of such smart parrots solving puzzles and learning complex concepts proves to humans is that we require attention and interaction in addition to our fabulous foods, enclosures, play gyms, and foraging stations. We need activities to keep our minds, as well as our beaks, busy. A bored bird can get into trouble if the owner hasn't been trained to provide good, wholesome activities for the bird's agile mind. Our intelligence is attractive to a lot of humans. But we have something else they want to see blossom from within us: our cuteness.

Sure, it may seem beneath you sometimes, but you really do need to sit on your human's hand or knee from time to time and just be your adorable self. At least let your human scratch your neck. Some humans are useful at helping break the sheathes on those itchy pin feathers, which come in when we're molting. That's a yearly change of the feathers that will make you fussy and squawky. If your human is willing to help you with the pin feathers, then, by all means, accept her help.

I write this for all the birds reading along because your cuteness matters as much as your intelligence. Your human thinks you're cute. Play that up!

You may be reading this as a newly fledged bird. Or you may be coming from a long life with a single owner you adored. Or you may have been with a terrible person who was mean or neglectful. But your new owner probably wants to love on you. If you're lucky, this person will give you the time you need to get used to a new home, surroundings, sounds, smells, lights coming from new areas, and all the foreign aspects before trying to give you neck scratches, but remember this person is offering *good* new stuff. Right? Use that smart bird brain to process all the novelty calmly and quietly in your new day cage. And keep being cute.

Chapter 2
The Story of the Egg

My bird parents created me, and I developed inside a shell for almost twenty-five days. You probably know that female birds—called hens—lay eggs. Because I'm a male bird, I won't lay an egg. As avian veterinarians have written and reported, laying an egg takes and uses calcium that would otherwise be used for the female's bones. Literally.

Additionally, if a female bird has an egg inside her that breaks or tears, releasing all the fluids and proteins from the egg into her body, she can suffer what the veterinarians call "yolk stroke." She has a stroke from the rush of proteins her body absorbs and can die if she doesn't get immediate veterinary care.

This is one of the reasons it's crucial for humans to make sure they know whether they have a female or male bird. If your human knows you're a girl, she can prepare for any calcium deficiencies or egg-related problems you might have during your life. For example, if you're a girl and your human notices you picking at your left leg suddenly, your human can whisk you off to the vet to make sure you don't have an egg stuck inside. That is a dangerous situation. (And it's the left leg that signals the problem.)

Think about chickens. When the hen lays too many eggs, she can get pathological bone weakness, which some researchers in the United Kingdom compared to osteoporosis in people. When all your calcium leaves your bones to go into making eggshells, your bones get brittle and can break. At the end of last century, the researchers in the United Kingdom learned that thirty-five percent of the caged hens that died during the laying cycle of their study died because of having fragile bones.

Obviously, we parrots are far superior to chickens. We are awesome birds. But we still have hollow bones and we still have to watch our mineral intake. See, you might be thinking it's a good idea to have your human add calcium to your food, whether you're a boy or a girl, just to be on the safe side. That's not entirely safe.

In the book "Mineral Tolerance of Domestic Animals" from the National Research Council, the researchers write in the chapter on Toxicosis:

> Phosphorus is involved in almost all aspects of metabolism. In addition, it interacts with many of the other essential and nonessential mineral elements making dietary levels of this element critical to optimum animal performance (growth rate, feed efficiency...egg production).
>
> Optimum animal performance is linked very closely with optimum calcium and phosphorus levels in the diet. Most animals require a fairly narrow calcium to phosphorus ratio—usually no wider than 2:1...A relative excess of phosphorus in relation to calcium can result in some very detrimental situations.

The chapter lists kidney and bladder stones, osteoporosis, and other bad things from having too much phosphorus and not enough calcium in your diet. "Thus, pronounced bone loss in adult animals can occur by feeding excess dietary phosphorus or insufficient dietary calcium. In some instances, the demineralized skeleton is replaced by fibrous connective tissue."

Because I'm a gorgeous parrot and not a scientific researcher, I'm not the right bird to list all the grams of minerals each species should take in. I just know it's important to have your human check that out and make sure your body has all the vitamins and minerals you need to be healthy.

When I was in the egg, my bird mom and bird dad took turns sitting on my egg to keep me warm so I could develop nicely. In the egg, all the nutrients I needed came to me through the yolk. When I think of it now, it grosses me out.

I don't like wet stuff to touch me. I have fabulous feathers, you see. I don't like to have messy things touch them. When I was in the egg, I didn't have feathers yet, and the warm, wet, gooey stuff was comfortable.

My story of the egg is a pleasant one. Sandy has told each of the birds in our little flock that we can share our egg stories with her, if we wish to. I mutter and chatter my story to her, but I'm not sure how much she understands of my native bird tongue. I think she understands that the egg was a small, safe place for me; it held me closely in a warm bath of nourishment until my body told me it was time to break free.

To hatch, I used what's called an egg tooth to create the first crack in the shell's defenses.

It took many hours to get free of the shell. I peeped and beeped and cheeped for my bird mom's help, but parrot parents are very wise. They knew I had to overcome the challenge on my own. It was the first test of my bird life. A parrot who can break out of his own egg will be strong enough to lift his head, to accept food, to move his wings, and so on. I have grown into the strong and formidable bird of awesomeness you see today because I overcame the challenge of hatching all on my own.

I have since taught Sandy not to put warm, wet, gooey stuff in my food dishes. And that's our next topic. How to train your human.

24

Chapter 3
How to Train Your Human
Selecting Your Favorite Song

If you have a good human, he or she will sing to you for your amusement and to show love for you. It took a while for Sandy to discover my favorite song, but I enjoyed the litany of tunes she went through over the years until she stumbled upon the right one. When your human sings something you don't like, I recommend emitting a series of high-pitched, short screams that reverberate off the walls like concussive forces. If you can shriek loudly enough in fast enough repetition, you can get your human to stop whatever he or she is doing.

I call this the CFS—concussive force shriek. This is not to be confused with a mere lesser shriek of dismay (LSD), which is exactly what it reads like—a lesser squawk. It usually takes a series of three to four CFSs to halt a human's behavior fully.

When your human sings something you like, I recommend swaying gently on the perch while offering kissing sounds. You may wish to whistle along with the tune if you know it—or even if you don't.

At our tree, Sandy sings "You Are My Sunshine" to me and I offer her kissing sounds as a reward.

We also have a bird at our tree who came from a frightening situation in Georgia. Her name is Bobo, and she likes to have Sandy sing "Somewhere Over the Rainbow." Even though Sandy screws up the words, Bobo will stare at her in amazement throughout the performance. We're convinced Bobo never thought she'd hear the song again after the ordeal she went through, and we'll talk about scary ordeals some birds have to overcome in another chapter.

One of the things your human might do for you, which you can encourage or discourage, is change the words of songs on purpose. Sandy tries to get one of the birds in our tree to sing, "I'm gorgeous and I know it," to some kind of rap tune. I think it's ridiculous, but she seems entertained by herself, and it makes the grey birds dance, so I sit back on my perch and watch the insanity. One you might try your beak with is this:

> *"I like cute birds and I cannot lie*
> *You other birdies can't deny*
> *When a bird flies in with his itty bitty toes*
> *And a big beak near your nose*
> *You get loud!"*

Again, I'm not saying this stuff is poetic, but Sandy gets the grey birds to dance with it.

Requesting a Bath Bowl
(with a clean-air discussion)

Because we're parrots, it's vital we keep our feathers in top flight condition. There are dusty birds like the African grey and the cockatoo *(Cacatua)* who actually create a substance called powder-down to protect their feathers.

Conures like myself don't have that, but when Sandy brought a couple of African greys into our tree a few years back, she also bought an air filter from the RabbitAir company, headquartered in California, that is designed specifically to clean the air I breathe. It works very well for this purpose. Sandy cleans the filter and vacuums its parts once a month, then, she changes the filter panels and cleans the whole contraption thoroughly twice a year. She says this is so she can feel confident she's keeping the air extra clean for us in the humid, tropical climate where we live.

She keeps track of our air because our bodies have highly specialized air sacs and lungs inside them. Even our bones allow air to flow through them. Our sensitive breathing systems can't have ionized particles bebopping through them or the smoke from nicotine cigarettes or the poison droplets from air fresheners. In fact, if a person in your tree smokes, you need to release a CFS at the person repeatedly until the person goes outside to do his or her smoking.

You need to make a rule that there is no smoking around birds. And if your person decides to install air fresheners or melt those smelly wax blocks to mask the smell of the smoke, release another CFS. Keep up the CFSs until all air fresheners and wax melting stops. Those things can kill birds. They release all kinds of poisonous droplets of tiny death bombs into the air and you, as the bird, breathe them in. They get stuck in your air sacs and scar your tissues.

Let me tell you how our lungs and air sacs work.

First, the air sacs range throughout a bird's body. We have air sacs in addition to lungs, and the sacs extend into our hollow bones. You can see diagrams of our respiratory system here:

http://people.eku.edu/ritchisong/birdrespiration.html.

When a bird inhales through his nares, most of the air goes into his caudal air sacs, with a bit going on through the caudal air sacs to the lung. Then he exhales air through the ventrobronchi and dorsobronchi, which divide into smaller-diameter air capillaries where little blood capillaries are flowing around and performing the oxygen and carbon dioxide exchange.

When the bird inhales a second time, the air travels from the capillaries to the cranial air sacs. Then he exhales a second time and the air travels out of the cranial air sacs and back out the nares.

In other words, the parrot's respiratory cycle requires us to inhale twice and exhale twice. The exchange of oxygen and carbon dioxide takes place in the walls of air capillaries, making the slow, deliberate respiratory system of birds a delicate one.

Another air danger comes from the kitchen. Older baking and cooking utensils in your tree could be coated with non-stick surfaces. This is supposed to make cooking and cleaning easier for a human, but it can also make cooking deadly for the birds in the tree. Make sure your human does not use Teflon™ cookware in your tree. Non-stick pots, pans, drip pans, oven liners, crockpot liners, foils, heating surfaces, carpet cleaners, irons, hair dryers, and more, often contain Polytetrafluoroethylene (PTFE) and/or Perfluorooctanoic acid (PFOA). These items emit fumes when heated and those fumes typically kill birds. It's not always a fast death, either. It's not painless. It's horrible and I'm writing this warning to help you avoid this tragedy in your tree.

Don't let your human risk it. Don't watch your human open a window to air out the kitchen while using an old skillet she's used before, so she thinks it's safe. If your human turns on the self-cleaning feature of the oven, let out a CFS and fly to the far end of the house, shrieking all the way. Self-cleaning ovens heat up to amazing temperatures and release horrible fumes that will kill you. Don't let your human use this feature on the oven. Ever.

Your human may need to remove all kinds of chemicals and cleaners from the tree once you're part of the flock. Our specialized air sacs just can't handle the droplets of poison that zing through the air.

A nice way for your human to keep dust and dander—like the wacky dander from African grey parrots and cockatoos—from getting into your respiratory system is to change tray papers on a daily basis and to wipe down dusty, feathery, poopy areas. Clean birds are healthy birds.

You'll want to let out a CFS if you see your human using funky chemicals to do any of the wiping, though. There are bird-safe cleaners on the market your human can pay lots of money to buy and use. Or your human can make some less-pricy cleaners from benign, organic products. Here are a few examples:

Bird-Safe Produce Wash
To clean the vegetables your human buys, she should make a bird-safe produce wash with these items:
- 1 tablespoon pink Himalayan salt
- 1 lemon
- ¼ cup raw apple cider vinegar

Here are the directions for her to follow:

Fill the sink with enough ice-cold water that the produce can float in it. Cut the lemon in half and squeeze as much of the juice over the top of the produce as you can. Then mix in a tablespoon of pink Himalayan salt. For the chemists reading, you may recognize that sounds like a diluted Hydrochloric acid (HCL). Yes. Yes, it is. Then add the quarter cup of raw apple cider vinegar. Swish everything around nicely and let it all soak for twelve to fifteen minutes before you drain the water. The last step is to rinse everything off and scrub any veggies that have dirt/mud or yucky stuff on them. The point of any produce wash is to get poisons and waxes off before you chop that into a mix or recipe for the feathered family.

Let's say your human needs to freshen the places where she sits around watching television. Don't let her use an aerosol product. In fact, read between the lines of popular air fresheners and air cleaners; they may not state outright that they kill birds, but you can find evidence of the fact. Instead, encourage your human to make her own upholstery cleaner with this simple method.

Bird-Safe Upholstery Cleaner
- 1 cup baking soda
- 3 to 4 drops lavender essential oil

Here are the directions for her to follow:
Remove your companion parrots from the area where you'll be cleaning furniture or freshening a mattress so stray baking soda and dangerous essential oils don't get into nares or air sacs. Combine the cup of baking soda and essential oil drops in a jar. Using a mesh strainer, sprinkle the concoction over the sofa, mattress, chair, or other fabric-covered surface. Let it sit for about one hour, and then thoroughly vacuum the sofa, mattress, chair, and so on. In the case of a cleaned mattress, replace clean sheets and have sweet dreams.

You can also share this recipe for a bird-safe glass cleaner.

Bird-Safe Glass Cleaner
- 1 cup white vinegar
- 3 cups distilled water
- 1 plastic spray bottle

Here are the directions for her to follow:

Begin by labeling the spray bottle so you always know which bottle is for your glass cleaner. Combine the cup of white vinegar with the distilled water in the spray bottle and shake well. Spritz the concoction onto a paper towel or blank newsprint paper and wipe down windows for a streak-free surface. Sandy recommends the paper towel when cleaning surfaces such as the front of the oven, refrigerator, microwave, and such surfaces.

To give the glass cleaner a sharper edge, add a teaspoon of baking soda and shake the bottle well. This gives you a floor cleaner with more punch than the mere glass cleaner, but you'll want a larger amount to work with. You can triple all ingredients, mixing them in a bucket, and use a scrub brush to get at cage bottoms, floors, and more without fearing the effects of scary chemicals. It's still smart to remove pet birds from the room while you're cleaning.

When in doubt, your human needs to throw out PFOA-coated products such as irons, curling irons, ironing board covers, drip pans from the back of the oven, old pressure cookers no one has used for years, and other items they can't verify as safe. Your life is more valuable than the price of a new skillet or saucepan. For example, when Sandy took us birds to our grandparents' house during a hurricane event, she and Grandma went to the store to buy bird-friendly pans in which to cook while we were camping there.

A few products Sandy recommends:
- Stainless steel pots and pans
- Cast iron skillets and pans
- Post-2017 cookware that states clearly it is PFOA-free

Another way Sandy keeps our air free of dust and dander is with regular bathing. She offers us baths all the time, but sometimes I have to *request* the bath bowl.

Bathing is important, not just so I can be the glorious and beautiful specimen of conure you see today. It also helps keep dustiness down for the greys in our tree. It also keeps Cricket, the green-cheek conure *(Pyrrhura molinae)*, from losing her mind. That little green bird is convinced she has to take a bath every single day. I only take a bath when I feel like it, so it's important Sandy understands when I'm asking for a bath bowl. Here's how I trained her on that.

I go to my water bottle where my drinking water sits. I tap on the nozzle with my fabulous beak of death. Then I look at Sandy and squawk once a noise similar to the human word for "bath."

If she's paying attention, Sandy knows that means it's time to fetch my special bowl and fill it with bottled water. If she's not paying attention, I have to go through the steps again, which is frustrating. There may come a point where I have to use a CFS or two to get her attention, then go through the steps.

Some birds prefer to bathe under the running water of a faucet. I think this is ridiculous. Sandy says there's nothing wrong with bathing under a faucet if your human is helping you, but I think this is awful. You're getting tap water on your feathers. Tap water. From God knows where. Do you know what's in the humans' tap water? Eew.

Some birds—the male Eclectus *(Eclectus roratus)* in our flock, in fact—like to bathe in the human shower. I think this is also ridiculous, but Sandy thinks it's cute. She says there are ways to make this safe for parrots. For example, if you want to bathe in the human shower, you need to have a sturdy shower perch that is low to the shower floor. The kind of perches that stick to the wall have been known to lose their suction and fall if your human hasn't glued them in place. Guess what happens to you if you're sitting on the perch when it falls. Birdie mayhem. I'm not fond of birdie mayhem.

Some birds like to bathe in their water bowls. I think that's disgusting, but I've seen it. If you want to bathe in your drinking water, that's your prerogative, but please make sure your human is aware of your bizarre tendencies and changes your water after you've had your dirty feet and cloacal opening in it. And before you drink from it.

There are also birds out there who like to have water sprayed on them. Sandy tried this with me a couple of times. It only took a few CFSs to train her against that.

She tried spraying the water upward, above my head, and telling me, "Oh, look, Petri, it's raining!" As much as I appreciate her trying to entertain me, I did not appreciate water droplets falling on my head. I'm an indoor bird who doesn't tolerate rain.

We didn't do that again, but there are some birds who like it. If you're one of them, see if you can get your human to do the "raining" thing. It was interesting to see Sandy at least try. (As a side note, make sure the spraying water comes from a bird-safe and clean container.)

Something to make sure your human avoids is shampoo and soaps. We birds are incredibly efficient at keeping our feathers clean. We have an upygial gland from which we grab a dab of special oil onto the tip of the beak, and then we run that oil along our feathers. Each day, we preen for an average of three total hours, cleaning each feather so that we are always flight ready. (This also distributes our signature scent, which is useful for attracting a mate or making your human hyperventilate sniffing you. It may seem "odd" to have your owner sniff your feathers, but it's something humans do. You'll get used to the adoration.)

Putting shampoo on a parrot disrupts the delicate balance of the gland's oil and puts us in danger of being poisoned. Shampoo and soap can dry our skin and cause allergic reactions if it doesn't outright poison or kill us. If you see your owner mixing up some kind of shampoo for your bath bowl, break out a steady stream of CFSs. Don't take a dip in that mess. Instead, dump the bowl over and poop on it from a high perch.

And while we're speaking of being flight ready, be cautious when you preen your human's hair. Sandy lets me preen her hair because she doesn't put any product in it. If your human puts strange stuff like mousse, gel, leave-in conditioner, or hair spray in his or her hair, you don't want to get that poison in your beak or on your tongue.

Eyeglasses: Perching vs. Tugging
Some humans wear eyeglasses. These can make interesting perches for a bird of diminutive size—like the sixty-five-gram green-cheek conure I live with or a tiny parrotlet. For a bird of my awesomeness, eyeglasses are a bit too small for perching safely. Instead, I use Sandy's glasses for communication.

When seated on your human's shoulder, you can tug on her glasses in a calm, gentle manner to get her attention for neck scratches. Just give a little tug with your beak. When she reaches up to re-adjust the glasses, scoot your head and neck into position to intercept the fingers.

The gentle tug is also a polite way to remind your owner to share snacks with you. Keep in mind, she can't give you snacks that are high in sugar or salt, but there are plenty of other good noms you can remind her to give you access to.

I give a firmer tug-of-purpose when I need to use my perch to defecate. Because I'm a courteous bird, I don't poop on humans. Sandy appreciates this. While many parrots have "movements" about once every fifteen or twenty minutes, I'm perfectly capable of holding my vent closed longer than that.

Sandy monitors such things and doesn't make me sit uncomfortably. If she loses track of time, I give her glasses a firm tug-of-purpose and she carries me to my perch. Now, be aware, your human may say silly things to you, as Sandy does. I have to endure the repeated question, "Do you need to do your poopies?" or "Is it time for your poopies on your perch?" until she gets me to the perch.

The end result is, I get to perform my droppings and relax myself, return to her shoulder, and there's no mess.

Why Fly When You Can Ride?

You may have noticed in that discussion of training your glasses-wearing human that I have Sandy carry me around. I am perfectly capable of flight. Sandy allows the parrots in our little flock to fly because we are birds who need to keep our chest muscles working properly. She takes precautions to keep us safe, of course, and we'll chat about that in just a second, but I want to make it clear to you refined parrots that you can have your human carry you around. You don't have to work.

Sandy knows my tug-of-purpose on her glasses means I'm in need of my perch. She knows my slight nip of her ear means I'm tired and ready for my cozy hut for bedtime. She has taken her training seriously over the years. By communicating with her in gentle, calm ways, I get to be carried to perches and play stands without expending the energy of flying unless I want to.

When it comes to flying, make sure you know the difference between a window and the outside. You don't want to bonk into a glass panel and break a bone. Too many birds have flown at high speeds right into glass panels and broken themselves so badly, they have died. It's a sad, horrible reality for the human you leave behind to deal with, so you'll want to train your owner to make accommodations for you if you'll be flighted in your tree. For example, some people close blinds and curtains before letting parrots out for flying. They'll put a cover over mirrors so we don't get confused by the wacky reflections and accidentally bonk into that glass.

Make sure ceiling fans are off before you fly anywhere near them. The blades have been known to break wings and kill birds.

Also watch out for scary rooms when you're flying. Kitchens? I would just stay out of that room. While most treats can be found in the kitchen, you can train your human to bring treats out to you, thus you can avoid hot stoves, boiling water, a sink full of sudsy poison-water, sharp knives, and such things. Also avoid bathrooms. Oh my bird, do you know what's in the bathroom? Hot curling irons and scary, gross, open toilets. Hopefully your owner knows to keep toilet lids closed closed closed all the time when there's a parrot in the house, but it may be up to you to stay clear of that horrible, germ-ridden, watery death.

Chapter 4
Shirt Surfing and Other Extreme Contact Sports

When Sandy came to get me that first night all those years ago, Brenda gave her some advice. Brenda told her I would become accustomed to the number of hours she spent playing with me each day, so it would be in my best interest if Sandy exercised self-discipline and didn't spend *too* much time with me while I was a novelty to her. The idea was that some people get a new bird, spend a ton of time with the bird in the beginning of their relationship, then break the bird's heart when the novelty wears off and the human has other activities that take time away from what used to be playtime.

Let me suggest that you not let your human fall into that mindset. Sandy and I have overcome the early years of me being a perch potato and not wanting to be touched. I've learned it's wonderful when she gives me scratches on my neck. I've also discovered the awesomeness of shirt surfing.

Shirt surfing takes great skill. If your human tucks his shirt into his pants, you have a built-in safety net. If your human wears loose-fitting clothing, you could accidentally flop out the bottom of a shirt and have to flap wildly to keep from falling to the floor. This is undignified.

To surf a shirt, keep at least one point of contact with the cloth at all times. For example, grip a wadded-up bit of the shirt's hem in your left foot while dangling and spinning from your right. Or you could hold the collar in your beak while you rake your claws across a silky portion of the shirt to pretend you're ice skating in place. My favorite thing to do is duck down inside Sandy's shirt with my back against her neck. Then I can wedge myself between the cloth of her shirt and the skin of her body while I power my scooting action with my feet. This is much easier than trying to push your back along the cloth, using your toenails to pad along the skin. Your human is likely to object to that.

One sport you want to avoid is teeth-cleaning. Stay out of your person's mouth. I know that might sound self-explanatory, but there are some birds who get some sort of sick thrill out of grabbing table scraps from between their owner's teeth. Don't do this. It's gross.

A human's mouth has more germs than you can shake a stick at, and our naturally occurring birdie bacteria don't have the resources to combat those germs properly. You could end up sick and messed up digestively if you take food out of your person's mouth.

Now, this doesn't mean you can't exchange beakie kisses with your owner. Just be cautious that your human isn't doing something strange that would get drool all over your beak. Again, that's gross. Sandy is quite sweet when she places a nice little kiss on top of my beak or on top of my head. It's a lovely way for a human to show affection for us birds and she keeps drool out of the equation.

No matter what fun games you play with your human, the point is to play with your human. You don't want to be a perch potato. While, yes, there are times when you'll want to hang out, lean against your cozy hut, and chew on the end of a toy while watching television, you really don't want to make a habit of sitting and letting your muscles atrophy.

In fact, there's a yucky foot problem that can start if you stand incorrectly on your feet…and just stand…and stand…and stand. Big-word warning! It's called pododermatitis and it can eat away your feet, starting with pain from infection. Some people just call it "bumble foot" because that's easier to say. Sandy talked to a vet about the condition to write an article for bird owners. Here's what she learned:

> In companion parrot circles, we usually refer to the sores or lesions that can form on caged birds' feet as "bumble foot." If only one

foot or leg has symptoms, the bird probably has something other than bumble foot going wrong, but there are causes and cures for this malady.

Any parrot with a bacterial infection, dietary deficiency, or bad perching conditions could develop pododermatitis. According to birdvet.com, the most common species to develop the problem are "budgies, cockatiels, galahs, and ducks."

The first thing parrot owners want to do is create an environment where their birds are less likely to develop this painful swelling in the feet and legs. Then parrot owners want to know what to watch for.

First, offer a variety of perches. Avoid straight, metal perches. Avoid dowel rod perches. Avoid sand-coverings on perches. Also, make sure the enclosure has a clean "floor" where the bird does ground foraging. Bacteria can build up anywhere a surface is unclean, then move onto the foot that steps there. Corn cob and other substrates are breeding grounds for bacteria over which your feathered friend must sit, play, eat, sleep, and live. Opt for something easier to clean, such as butcher paper or packing paper you can purchase from a moving store.

Second, make sure your birds get good vitamin A through fresh foods in addition to their formulated pelleted foods. But keep in mind that fresh foods will be a breeding ground for bacteria if you leave them in the enclosure too long. Fresh offerings should be removed when they're turning no-longer-fresh.

M. Scott Echols, DVM, Diplomate ABVP, listed a few of the risk factors for bumble foot:
- Being overweight;
- Uneven weight bearing (such as standing on one leg, arthritis in one leg, deformed leg, etc); and
- Dowel rod perches (most common cause that he sees).

In the early stages of development, bumble foot will present as enflamed blisters on the bird's feet. If you notice the loss of scales on the bottom of your bird's feet, you may be able to reverse the problem by making simple husbandry changes such as softening perches with vet wrap and improving the diet.

The second stage begins after blisters have ruptured and sores appear. At this point, you must have an avian veterinarian step in to prescribe antibiotics and anti-inflammatories. Without veterinary care, the next stage could develop into distended and swollen ulcers that may split and ooze. Resolve the problem before this happens to your feathered friend.

Keep in mind, I've talked about the emergency times you'll need to go to the avian veterinarian, and Sandy's article talks about a special reason to go to the vet. As much as I don't like it, I must remind you to have your human take you to an avian veterinarian for an annual well-bird checkup. It sounds horrifying, I know. But it's important for a vet to establish your good, healthy baseline.

The trip will be annoying; I won't lie. And the vet will probably put a cotton swab in your crop to do a "culture." I don't know what's cultural about poking a stick down a parrot's throat, but there you have it. Crazy humans do crazy things to make sure we birds are happy and healthy, inside and out. The vet will determine what good and bad bacteria you have in that organ. The vet may also take some blood to count your blood cells and test different enzymes to make sure your liver, kidneys, and other organs function properly. Go with it and your human will probably give you a fabulous treat when the visit is over.

Chapter 5
Sometimes Humans are Difficult to Understand

How to Protect Yourself from Poisonous Foods

You will notice that humans do crazy things. One of the crazy things they do is eat poison. Chocolate and alcohol are the two strangest poisons I don't understand. Sandy used to be friends with a guy who needed a place to live, and he drank a lot of alcohol. He was mean to me and scared me so badly one night that I threw all my tail feathers out flying myself away from him.

(This is a good trick to remember if you're ever in a bad situation. We birds can throw our tail feathers to get away from danger. They'll grow back.)

Sandy got us away from that guy, thank goodness. But the alcohol poisoned him all the time. It was always stinky. If your human hangs out with someone who is always being poisoned by alcohol, chirp and mutter in your human's ear that you want to get away from that.

The alcohol itself is something you want to avoid. Don't drink a human's poison. There are stories of birds getting a beakful of beer and *not* dying, but there are far more stories of parrots drinking from humans' glasses of alcohol and getting sick.

One night, some pet owners partied with friends, drinking alcohol from pretty glasses that their parrots thought were bright and shiny. When the people fell asleep, the parrots consumed the attractive leftovers. Of course. We're curious creatures. The sad and tragic morning found the parrots dead from drinking alcohol. It's heartbreaking. Don't be one of those curious parrots who drinks poison.

Don't eat avocados, chocolate, raw onions, or any of the scary things on the list at this link:
   birdsupplies.com/pages/poisonous-foods-for-parrots

Other Evils in the Tree
I have a few lists of annoying—or flat out evil—things Sandy has subjected me to. Going to the vet scores high on the list. I also consider her use of the vacuum cleaner, travel cages, and cameras to be unnecessary, bordering on abusive at times. While I agree that I'm a gorgeous bird, worthy of posing for portraits, I fear large cameras with big flashes. Here are a few minor evils and the reasons why I find them irritating.

Top 10 Reasons Vacuums Are Evil
I'm not sure why humans think they need to run vacuum cleaners across the carpet all the time. Sandy runs hers around my cage about every other day. I don't get it. But she's convinced this is necessary.
10. Vacuums are huge. (but even the small Dust Buster that she uses on little messes is evil)
9. Vacuums suck up perfectly good food pellets I've dropped by accident.
8. Vacuums are ugly and hard machines that would never make good toys.
7. I heard a story of a canary getting sucked up in the hose of a vacuum—this is true—and it tore his feathers out—he died within hours. (His human was not exercising good judgment by cleaning his cage with the vacuum while he was in the cage.)
6. Vacuums have long tails that follow them around the house, trying to trip Sandy while she's working.
5. Vacuums are incredibly loud and scary.
4. Vacuums are incredibly loud and scary.
3. Vacuums are incredibly loud and scary.
2. Vacuums are incredibly loud and scary.
1. Vacuums are incredibly loud and scary.

Top 10 Reasons Travel Cages Are Evil
10. Travel cages do not have fun play gyms attached.
9. They are small and confining.
8. They usually have small-bird-body-size doors that are difficult to get in or out of. And I am a huge raptor.
7. They make different noises than normal cages when you tap your beak on them.
6. They don't hold the right toys in appropriate ways.
5. They don't hold the right food or water dishes in appropriate ways.
4. They don't always have a sanitary screen to separate you from your poop tray. (so disgusting)
3. Once you destroy one, your human will find a sturdier one for your next excursion.
2. Sometimes they take you to a babysitter's house, which means my mom is going away for several days. And that sucks.
1. They usually take you to bad places—like the vet.

Top 10 Reasons Cameras Are Evil
After reading this list, you'll agree, we birds should always hide behind our toys from cameras.
10. They come out of nowhere when you least expect them—usually when you're minding your own business playing with a new toy or eating a new treat.
9. The really big, really loud ones are stored at a place you have to ride in a travel cage to get to. (and we all know how horrible travel cages are) (those cameras also have big lights and scary umbrellas set up around them)
8. They cause Sandy to make quirky noises at me.
7. They cause strangers called "photographers" to make quirky noises at me.
6. They don't look like any toy I've ever played with.
5. They make a funny noise that no other device in the house makes.
4. The round part on the front of them moves of its own volition.

3. The little black doors on the round part move of their own volition (usually right before a blinding light).
2. They take away your eyesight for at least a full minute with their blinding flash of light.
1. They look a lot like cell phones, which are also evil.

Chapter 6
Relaxing in Safe Trees
Your Tree
One of the great things about getting your human trained early in your relationship is teaching him or her to give you space to relax. Sometimes you want to lean back on the perch and watch TV. Trust me, there are some bizarre things that flash across the screen in vivid color. If you get afraid of any of the things you see, give a good CFS and your owner will change the channel for you. When Coconut the Cockatiel *(Nymphicus hollandicus)* saw snakes on the television screen, she would flip out. Sandy learned to censor our TV viewing, so no snakes appeared on the screen. With no worry about snakes, television shows can be quite relaxing.

It's also nice to chirp and chatter along to the radio from inside a cozy hut. Here's the thing about cozy huts—they are snuggly, cozy, warm, and delightful, but they can be maddeningly dangerous. First, I haven't met a parrot yet who could resist customizing the hut to make it hold the body perfectly. In the past, Sandy purchased the huts made of the fuzzy material that tickled my mouth when I beaked it. But the stitches and threads of that kind of cozy proved dangerous. That stupid hut tried to kill me! The string grabbed my neck and wouldn't let go. I was hanging and turning in a circle when Mom reached into my cage to support me and help me. I was so freaked out that—I'm embarrassed to say it—I beaked her more than once while she got the string off my neck. Sandy won't allow that type of hut in our tree any longer.

Currently, Cricket and I have a different type of hut that we share. It has a flat floor that's more difficult for me to customize. Sandy is obsessive about it, which is frustrating at times. Just when I have a nice hole developed in an area where I can rest my adorable belly at night or during afternoon naps, she replaces the hut with a new, unembellished one.

    Sometimes the whole tree must change for a bit.

How to Evacuate with Minimal Stress
Sometimes humans have no warning about a bad situation. For example, if there's a fire in the tree, or a shake of the earth, your human may have to stuff you into a shirt—or, Heaven forbid, a pillowcase that she keeps under your cage—and run out of the burning or shaking place to keep you safe. While this would be frightening to put up with, you could endure it for the short time it lasted. Most of our owners have friends with birds who could bring a travel cage to you and let you hang out in the safe space while the humans take care of better arrangements for your optimum comfort.

    Sandy has heard non-pet-owning people complain about the idea of taking time to save a pet if a house is on fire, and Sandy considers those people wrong. Just wrong. She would have no reason to go on living if something terrible happened to us birds, and she knows other bird owners who feel the same. We are amazing creatures, after all. Stuffing one of us in a pillowcase may take ten or fifteen seconds, but that's ten or fifteen seconds the human will forever be thankful she committed to safeguarding you.

    Some bad situations *do* give enough warning for your human to get you and your special things ready for the inconvenience. For example, if you live in an area of the world where big snowstorms knock down your electrical power, your owner might need to set up birdie day camp near a safe, PFOA-free, and smoke-free fireplace. If you live in an area of the world where you experience hurricanes, your human might need to set up birdie day camp near a battery-operated fan that can keep you cool while you wait for the power grid to be restored.

    Before one of the hurricanes headed toward our tree, Sandy packed our flock into travel cages and took us to our grandparents' house to be safe. She had ample warning that the storm was coming, so she had time to make sure our travel cages and travel bags were perfect and ready to go. Here's what she says is best to have in an emergency cage.

- At least one perch;
- A secured food dish;
- A secured water dish or bottle;
- A toy that is secured so that it doesn't waggle and bump your bird during travel;
- A cover for the cage; and
- A cozy hut (if your bird is used to that) or something under which your bird can hide.

On the outside of the cage, where a nervous beak can't reach it, you need to have a label that lists your name; your owner's name, address, phone number, and email address; your veterinarian's name and phone number; and an emergency contact's name and phone number. This label is important in case something happens that separates you from your owner. Other people should be able to read it and get you back to your person.

In your emergency travel bag, your owner should put all the things you require for the duration of the event. Here's what Sandy recommends as a baseline travel bag list.

- Your non-perishable food;
- Treats;
- A bottle of water (or two);
- An emergency first-aid kit (corn starch to stop any minor bleeds, children's Benadryl to treat any allergies, vet wrap, scissors, etc.); and
- A copy of your medical file with your band number written down.

Chapter 7
Some Birds Live Through Scary Stuff

Traveling with Sandy has never been scary. She makes sure I have all the comforts of the tree wherever I go. But not all birds are so fortunate. I've mentioned a couple of times that Sandy brought birds into our flock from different situations; some of those situations were scary for the birds, while some were not. Here's an example of "not really scary."

Teka and Ernie's Story
Teka is an African grey parrot, which is another type of smart parrot. The lady who loved him had gotten so busy with work that she didn't have much time to spend playing with him. In fact, Teka had been living in a large, fabulous cage with an abundance of perches and toys on a screened-in lanai in sunny, warm, Southwest Florida, but he hadn't had out-of-cage playtime for several years. The lady who loved him recognized that pattern wasn't going to change, and she knew Teka needed more interaction and stimulation, so she looked for an owner who would cave to Teka's every whim. Basically, she looked for a human like mine.

One day, Sandy went to visit Teka and his cage mate, Ernie, taking them some yummy food and a couple simple foot toys she'd made, to see if the birds would accept either from her. Apparently, everything went "okay," because those two birds joined our flock a few weeks later.

When your human brings a bird to your home, you want the newcomer to be in quarantine for thirty to sixty days. (Dr. Branson Ritchie at the College of Veterinary Medicine at the University of Georgia says cockatiels hide certain illnesses so well that you should have them quarantined away from your main flock for up to ninety days.) You want the new bird to go through some tests at the vet to make sure he is healthy and not harboring any scary germs that might hurt you.

Sandy did this stuff with Teka and Ernie, of course. She's very protective of me. But we didn't realize Ernie had something sad happening in his body. Within a few months, she noticed Ernie was regurgitating an awful lot, as if trying to provide for his shiny bowls and toys. She took him to the vet to make sure he was okay.

He was not.

It was heartbreaking to watch Sandy caring for that big, green bird, but Ernie didn't live with us for more than ten months. He had a seizure and passed away in Sandy's arms while she showered his big, orange beak with kisses. It was a tremendously sad day.

The point is that Teka and Ernie didn't come from a terrible past the way some poor birds do.

Bobo's Story
For example, Bobo the Eclectus lived in disgusting, stinking conditions in the home of a cardiovascular surgeon in Georgia. If you look up the story online, you can find the court case of the doctor whom a judge ordered to have no more birds in that state. I learned that he had the title of "hoarder." Some people say that title with derision, when it's just a mental condition that makes it difficult for a person to let go of items. In fact, this man in Georgia collected and hoarded parrots of all types, and, in his case, even Sandy says the title with a snarl.

DeKalb County Animal Services invited staff from Ziggy's Haven Parrot Sanctuary in Inverness, Florida, to rescue as many birds as they could from the man's home. Bobo survived when many other birds died there. They died from lack of care. They died from lack of food. They died from lack of water. They died next to piles of defecation.

It's no wonder poor Bobo has trust issues. I try to stay away from her, so she never has a reason to bite me. Sandy, on the other hand, sings to Bobo and offers her a wide variety of yummy foods. She says we're going to give Bobo the best days of her life.

I think that's nice.

These are two ends of the spectrum for bringing a bird from one home to another. Teka and Ernie came from a family that loved them; they just didn't receive the attention a bird of our vast intelligence requires. Bobo was in a life-or-death situation from which she had to be removed, quarantined, restored, and helped.

Here's another example of scary things birds may have been through. Some humans keep a variety of pets in their homes. I've heard stories of dogs chasing and grabbing birds who are having their out-of-cage time. Dogs who were good friends with the bird suddenly noticed something feathery or quirky about their housemate, and their predatory, hunter instinct kicked in, to disastrous effect. I've heard stories of cats who reached through the bars of cages and frightened smaller birds into having heart attacks.

Even something as seemingly harmless as being licked by the family cat can kill a bird. Cat saliva is poisonous to birds, and if your human doesn't know this, you must be the responsible one who stays away from the pet cat. No matter how tempting it may be to play with the whiskers, don't do it!

Another scary thing that a bird might remember from his past is something he's seen happen to another bird. For example, Winston the Eclectus used to live with a veterinarian who provided him an outdoor aviary in Southwest Florida. It sounds swanky at first. Unfortunately, Winston saw a hawk poke its claws and beak through the wire of the aviary and kill his mate. He also saw racoons—those sneaky tricksters—work together to kill another cage mate. He has seen frightening things, and, for some reason, he's afraid of red trucks.

We may never know why he's afraid of red trucks, but Sandy has promised Winston that we'll never own one. He'll never have to ride in one as long as Sandy is caring for him, and she has this information included in his medical file, which we'll talk about in the next chapter.

Just keep in mind, new birds coming to your tree could have frightening memories that give them night frights. If one of the birds in your flock has night frights, you can learn to deal with that. Yes, it's obnoxious when the bird across the living room suddenly explodes in a cacophony of feathers and squawking and beating wings in the middle of the dark, quiet night, but you can be a calm, wise presence for him or her. Sandy keeps a night light in the living room for us birds because Winston and Bobo have bad memories that startle them awake sometimes.

You can train your human to keep a night light for you, if that helps. Or you can train your human to give you a darkening cover for your sleep cage to help block rustles of wind from fans or vents, or headlights from passing cars that dance across the ceiling when you least expect them. Use the CFS and other methods of communication to request what works best for you.

Bobo's method of communication is a glare of indignation. Sandy is certain Bobo thinks we're all crazy. So much so that she imagines Bobo keeps a running list of grievances. At least, these are "problems" in Bobo's opinion.

Bobo's List of Grievances
1. My Name. The Crazy Woman (TCW) tried to change my name when I first arrived here. I was literally FORCED to use my voice and tell her my name is Bobo to prevent her from calling me Clementine. *Clementine.*
2. Bath Bowl. I think my bath bowl should be larger. And I think it should have a platform for diving.
3. Privacy. TCW looks.at.my.droppings. She tells me when she's pleased with the color of my droppings. What kind of insanity is that?
4. Bananas. TCW only purchases three or four bananas at a time, thus she claims to "run out" after a few days. This is poor banana management on her part and needs to be rectified.

5. Schedules. TCW can't figure out which days I prefer my cranberries cut in half and which days I prefer them whole.
6. Mini Pumpkins. Why doesn't TCW offer mini pumpkins to me on a daily basis? While I might not be interested EVERYday, I would like that option.
7. Peas. TCW offered me WET, organic, English peas. It was disgusting. I only eat dry, dehydrated peas that I can beak the shells off.
8. Silly Foraging. TCW has the infuriating habit of hiding nutri-berries and mango YoDips around my cage so that I must find and collect them all to a central location for eating at my leisure. She also hides these treats around the jungle gym, resulting in the same obnoxious exercise for me. The most heinous foraging situation, though, was hiding cranberries in an artichoke-of-death. TCW placed a full, complete, frightening artichoke IN MY CAGE and expected me to find treats within it.
9. Mango YoDips. Why is there a limit of one per day?
10. My final grievance is that she takes none of this seriously!

Chapter 8
Everybirdie Needs a Medical File

I mentioned that Sandy has a medical file for Winston. In fact, she has a separate file for each of us birds.

At a convention where she gave a presentation one year, Sandy met a lady named Michelle Vrbka who makes these wonderful leather-bound notebooks for organizing the vital information you need to have with you throughout your bird life. Sandy was impressed with the level of detail Michelle had put into preparing the notebooks; they looked extremely professional and well thought out. You can check them out here:

www.bonzabird.com

Let's face it, some birds will live longer than our humans. Sandy worries about some of the birds outliving her and having to adapt to new situations and new people. (They'll have to retrain all the behaviors *she's* learned so well.) Our files are not as robust and fancy as the leather-bound notebook Michelle creates.

What Sandy made is a three-ring binder with a separate folder for each of us. I'll describe my folder since I'm the most important bird.

The Orange Folder

My folder is orange to match my most adorable fluffy feathers and top head feathers—the ones around my eyes especially. They are quite bright like fire, you know.

Anyway, my folder is orange. Inside the folder is a clear baggie sort of thing that Sandy calls a slipcover for paper. I don't know why paper needs to go in a covering, but she uses it to hold a few lovely pictures of me. As I've mentioned before, I don't like the process of having my picture taken. Cameras are evil. But the result is usually quite nice. Sandy also has some of the feathers I've molted in the slipcover. She also has two calendars in the slipcover because, yes, I am so awesome that two different organizations have chosen me as a calendar bird. (Sandy says this proves what excellent organizations they are.) Also, in the slipcover, she has the genetic test certificate that proves I'm a boy. (As if we needed proof of that.)

On one side of my medical folder, Sandy includes a typed list of my favorite foods, current dietary needs, any medications or supplements I'm taking, or any allergies she suspects I have. (Winston is allergic to chamomile, so he must avoid the unregulated teas that some avian community members were touting a few years back.)

She also puts my "eccentricities" and habits there. For example, when I become amorous in late January or February each year, I tend to get squawky. If I were a wild bird, I'd seek out a female to make eggs with. Sandy doesn't mind my squawking, and she'll offer me different foods to help calm my nerves. But if Sandy was suddenly not around, some less-trainable human might not understand I need fewer fresh fruits in February to tone down my hormonal reaction to the sugar. So my human has it written out.

On the other side of the notebook, she has all my health records. Veterinary printouts and receipts that show dates of vet visits, my weight history, medicines I've taken and when, go there. She even has notes about my droppings in there, which is a little embarrassing. But it's all so she's prepared if I get sick, or so anyone can step in and help me if something terrible happens to her.

Now, let's get serious for a minute.

We all know parrots live a long time. We are long-lived companion pets. That's why Michelle (and Sandy) created notebooks to track the health and needs of birds. When Teka and Ernie came to live with us, Sandy didn't receive any health records for either of them. She was at a loss when Ernie got sick. Ernie didn't even have a leg band that she could use to find his earliest information.

That's one of the reasons Sandy is a proponent of keeping your leg band. It's a nice piece of jewelry that proves you belong to a human and deserve pampering. But it's also a wealth of information if the right human or veterinarian looks up the numbers on the band.

If you get to a point where your leg band is obtrusive or you tend to get it caught in toys, your owner can have a veterinarian remove it (carefully), but make sure it stays with your medical file. Don't lose that nugget of information!

Another thing Sandy is big on is weighing us. She bought a kitchen scale that can weigh in grams and bought a light-weight T-perch that sits atop the scale. Once a week, she cajoles us to take turns standing on the perch, records our weights, and gives us a treat for being cooperative. (Bobo has yet to be cooperative, and Sandy says that's okay for now.)

The reason for tracking our weight in this manner is to track our health. You see, we birds are masterful at hiding when something is wrong with us. I mean, nobirdie wants to reveal a weakness.

Our wild cousins living out in the scary world can get picked off by a predator if they're looking sickly. Sometimes, a flock in the wild will leave a sick bird behind by himself, which I think is sad. There are some types of birds who will kill off a sick member of the flock, which, again, terrifies me.

Because it's dangerous to show signs of illness, we birds are good at hiding the signs. The humans who care for us must be good at noticing every tiny symptom we might let slip, or else they'll not know we're sick until we're *extremely* sick. Sandy is amazing at noticing when we have a problem. It's like she's in tune with our immune systems or something. Cricket sneezed one day, and a fleck of dirt spewed out of one of her nares. Sandy packed her into the emergency carrier and took her to the vet that very day. Cricket told me about the vet flushing her nose to dislodge any particulates, and it sounded horrible to me. But this is the kind of caution a human needs to use when watching for signs of illness.

One thing Sandy does to watch for symptoms is weighing us. If a small bird—like Cricket—loses five or six grams overnight, you need to pay attention and see if that is a fluke, or if the bird is getting sick.

The rule of beak is this: a large bird could lose up to ten percent body weight in a week's time without too much worry, but at ten percent, your human should give the vet a call and chat about what's going on. A small bird could lose up to five percent body weight in a week's time without too much worry, but at five percent, your human should give the vet a call and chat about what's going on.

Notice that I'm not suggesting your human cram you into a travel carrier and run you to the vet's office because you lost five grams in a week. Can you imagine? Some birds have morning droppings that weigh five grams. You'd end up learning to hold your droppings in if your human took you to the vet every time you had a large one. And that's no good.

Sandy tells me I'm pleasantly plump at one-hundred and twenty-six grams. This is slightly heavier than the one-hundred and twelve to one-hundred and twenty grams that sun conures typically weigh. She says this is all right with her because it gives me room to lose weight if I want. It also gives me room to deal with the effects of antibiotics. I understand the concept there, although veterinarians would probably scowl at her. You see, when I took antibiotics at eighteen years old, they made me feel queasy, and I lost a few grams. Sandy says the extra weight I have is like a buffer. (Chapter One has some good websites listed, but here's one where avian veterinarian Dr. Scott McDonald researched real-world best weights for companion parrots. Visit http://www.scottemcdonald.com/pdfs/Average%20Weights.pdf.)

The fat bird in our tree is Winston the Eclectus. He doesn't like to stand on the scale perch because Sandy usually announces, "Oh my, Winston, you need to exercise more." Then Winston must climb over obstacle courses she builds in the living room floor and he receives smaller portions of birdie bread when Sandy's handing out treats. Feeding Winston isn't easy because he's an Eclectus.

The Fragile Eclectus
When Sandy published a pet bird magazine, she interviewed an Australian avian veterinarian who had performed field research to study the feeding habits of the Eclectus parrot. With his permission and help, she prepared an article titled "Here's How to Feed the Eclectus Parrot in Human Care," which detailed his findings and dietary suggestions. Here is an edited version of that article from Spring 2017.

> Owners of Eclectus parrots (*Eclectus roratus*) know these birds have different dietary needs than have other parrots. One of the well-known reasons for the specialized-diet conversation is the different gastro-intestinal system Eclectus parrots have when compared to other psittacines. Rob Marshall B.V.Sc., M.A.C.V.Sc. (Avian Health) at Carlingford Animal Hospital in New South Wales, Australia, shared the key features of Eclectus digestion:
> - A large crop size;
> - A wide thoracic esophagus;
> - A highly elastic and spacious proventriculus, which allows food much time to linger in it;
> - Short food-passage time in the gizzard;
> - Rapid movement of food through the small intestine after leaving the gizzard; and
> - Highly regulated crop emptying.
>
> Gastric function is key to healthy digestion in these parrots, so one must look at the physical and chemical disintegration of food as it goes through the three stages of protein digestion. This will show the science behind the field observations supporting Marshall's recommendations for feeding the Eclectus in human care.

Marshall's research of wild Eclectus offers valuable observations of behavior that not only reveal tips for what to feed the Eclectus in human care, the observations also reveal tips for *how* to offer these foods. It all makes even more sense when we look inside the bird.

First, Marshall pointed out, food goes through the cephalic phase. As food enters the proventriculus from the crop, the proventriculus fills with peptic enzymes to help break down protein molecules before sending food to the gizzard. One of Marshall's presentations shows Pepsin and food filling the proventriculus together.

Second, Marshall pointed out, food goes through the gastric phase. As food enters the ventriculus—also called the gizzard or hind stomach—the ventriculus fills with Hydrochloric acid (HCL) to denature the protein bonds in the food.

One of the intriguing habits Marshall and his colleagues witnessed in the field, and something Eclectus parrot owners have commented on, is the way these parrots consume seeds. The astute owner will notice the Eclectus spending considerable time munching and crunching seeds and arils before consuming them.

Marshall explained to readers what they're seeing: "They break the seed into smaller pieces, better exposing them to stomach acids, which reduces the workload of the gizzard. The gizzard in Eclectus is prone to overload because it has evolved on a soft food wild diet of fruit pulp."

Third, food goes through the intestinal phase. Fast transit time and advanced protein digestion indicate a healthy digestive system. Marshall pointed out: "In clinical practice, functional digestive problems are encountered far more frequently in Eclectus than other parrot species."

Eclectus parrot owners can tell their birds may be experiencing digestive problems when they see the typical health clues. Look for changes in droppings and dropping consistency. If the first morning dropping has bubbles and/or extra water, it's time to make a veterinary appointment. Marshall states that feather stress bars, discoloration, and loss are signs of chronic digestive disfunction. If your Eclectus parrot is plucking and barbering his or her feathers, don't assume the problem is mere stress or boredom. Look at digestive health. Take your bird to the vet and discuss real Eclectus dietary needs.

"Ninety-five percent of feather destruction behaviors in Eclectus have a physical base," Marshall shared. "Digestion dysfunction is the most common cause of feather destruction. This must be identified and resolved in the early stages before the destructive actions become habituated. They become habituated largely because the owners tell the birds to stop picking when they see the self-destruct, which causes an attention-seeking behavioral problem. Habituation occurs in birds that are sedentary and lack exercise, so their focus is on feather picking, which becomes a habit. Therefore, the feather destruction problem has physical and behavioral aspects. Even so, the feather destruction behavior will persist if the underlying cause is not attended to.

These behaviors are definitely not related to boredom or misdirected foraging behavior."

Let's look to the field research to see naturally occurring foraging behavior, and to learn more about the wild population's dietary practices.

The family tree is the focal point of Eclectus life with the female showing an urgent need to protect the nest. She will stay at the nest site while a group of males goes out to forage twice a day and return with food for her. While studying Eclectus in the wild, Marshall and colleagues investigated the wild diet and feeding habits of a family group of three males and one female of the Australian subspecies (*E. roratus macgillivray*) found in the lowland rainforests of Iron Range on Cape York Peninsula, Australia.

They observed the three males leave the family's Kajoolaboo tree (*Tetrameles nudiflora*) together at first light to forage along the Claudie River. One broke away from the mini group to forage near the shoreline while the other two flew ahead. All three returned within a reasonable timespan of one another to the family tree. In the afternoon, all three went foraging together again. The next morning, at first light, they were off again, soaring into the forest canopy to find breakfast.

Marshall stated this wild feeding behavior is highly regular, intermittent and offers enhanced protein digestion for the Eclectus parrot's unique digestive system. For healthy digestion, these birds in human care must follow a similar morning and afternoon mealtime routine.

He explained: "In the wild, Eclectus will fill their crops with food over a period of an hour or so in the morning. They eat on an empty stomach. The food eaten during this time will fill up the stomach and stretch it to capacity, which is critical to the gastric secretion of Hydrochloric acid and Pepsin. In the evening, the crop and stomach have emptied of food and the same process of digestions follows according to the principles of gastric secretion. Ultimately, this produces a fast transit time of food through the gut, which underpins their healthy digestive function."

Where owners often go wrong, Marshall pointed out, is in feeding foods that "reduce the rate of food passage through the gut, which predisposes Eclectus to many complicated digestion disorders.

"In our study, Eclectus parrots were seen eating succulent pulp from the fruit of *Salacia chinensis* and *Leea indica*. The textural qualities, water and nutrient content of these fruits are typical of canopy foods eaten by Eclectus parrots, which make up the bulk of their natural diet."

In our homes, Marshall pointed out, "Eclectus parrots are commonly fed according to granivory, which explains their high incidence of diet-induced digestive problems. Such problems are averted and remedied by adopting feeding schedules that better suit a digestion model weighted towards frugivory."

Marshall explained: "Cultivated fruits lack the nutritional richness of rainforest fruits. Therefore, we move towards cooked vegetables as a source of nutrients, and these are cooked to provide the functional requirements for healthy digestion in Eclectus. The foundation vegetables for Eclectus are cooked butternut pumpkin (squash), sweet potato, boiled rice, and cooked legumes. On top of these, we place fleshy commercially grown papaya, mango, passionfruit, pomegranate, kiwi fruit, and dragonfruit. But these are sources of vitamins and microminerals rather than major minerals and functional foods.

"In addition, you can add green beans, kale, carrot, and corn as foraging foods."

Chapter 9
Sometimes Ya Gotta Pluck

Plucking your feathers tends to send the humans in your midst into a frenzy. If you want extra attention, the best and quickest way to get it is the CFS, of course. But the next best thing is to pull out a pretty feather and play with it. Squish it around in your beak, pretend to have a great interest in the feather shaft. You may need to pluck several feathers and leave them in a pile on the bottom of your cage. That is a sure-fire way to make your owner freak out.

When Teka and Ernie first came to live with us, I was disappointed. Sandy brought their huge cage into the tree, and the two birds didn't act like they wanted to befriend any of us. Sandy also had a moron for a boyfriend at the time, and I didn't like the way he smelled of poison alcohol. So, I pulled out all the feathers on one of my legs and on my belly next to my leg. It took about forty-eight hours to do because I didn't do it all at once.

Sandy lost her mind. I received all the attention. In fact, she was going on a short, overnight trip, and I got to go with her. No boyfriend, no other birds, no distractions. Just my human and me. It was great.

Now, be aware that your owner might buy a soothing spray to spritz on the area you pluck. This might be cold against your skin, and this is obnoxious.

Sandy sought the advice of the veterinarian, of course. The vet took some of my blood to make sure I didn't have any kind of infection or problem going on inside me, which, seriously, I tried to tell them was the case. But it came down to this: I was stressed over the changes in our tree.

The vet recommended the soothing spray. Sandy bought it. I hated it. I hated it so much, that each time she saw me pick at the new feathers coming in and offered to spritz me with the soothing spray, I just stopped picking at the new feathers. I mean, I'd rather be a little itchy than have her notice my itchiness and try to solve it with that cold mess.

Now, Winston's feather-plucking is something different. Winston does the type of plucking that a lot of parrots do, and you might know a bird with this problem.

Habitual plucking.

Winston has seen some scary stuff, and has lived in several environments in his life. Before he came to live with our flock, he spent a year or so in a store and was going to be adopted by the owner of the store. The store's owner moved to a sanctuary out west, leaving Winston behind, so Sandy adopted him instead. This means Winston has a steady human now, but he has been plucking for many years.

He has certain times of the year when he lets green feathers grow, but typically he pulls them out so that his chest and belly are fluffy white feathers most of the time. To ensure he doesn't cause damage to his skin, Sandy makes sure he has plenty of shreddable toys to work on in his cage and on the play gyms. There are different textures to the shreddable things he works on so he can pick at things other than his wings and body.

A few years ago, she tried to put a leather collar around his neck so he wouldn't be able to reach his belly feathers with his beak. Winston did not appreciate that collar. It was too big for him and restricted his climbing ability. Sandy also tried something called a sock buddy, which is a person's sock with holes cut in it, so it fits over a bird's body but lets the wings poke through. It looked constricting from where I sat on my perch. I think it took Winston an hour to chew through it. He's a determined bird when he wants to be.

Birdonally, I recommend you not chew on your feathers. But if you must, try not to hurt yourself. There are some birds who will pluck and pick at an area on their bodies until they cause a sore that bleeds. If you do this, your owner should take you to the vet to determine what's going on. You may have something medically wrong inside that you're trying to get to, and you might not even realize it. Often, female birds will pick at their left leg and lower left belly area when they have an egg stuck. That's something the vet *really* must help with.

Sometimes, if you have an infection under your skin, you'll want to pick the feathers away. Your human should whisk you to the vet to get that fixed.

Of course, it's horrifying to go to the vet. Those doctors poke thermometers in your vent and place cold stethoscopes on your belly. As I've mentioned before, sometimes they swab cottony sticks in your throat. But once the indignities are over, they just might do something that helps you feel all better. And you can stop plucking your feathers.

Chapter 10
Your Human Will Cook for You

On the market today, you'll see several formulated diets designed to tempt our beaks with flavors and textures. Many of them are crap, in my birdie opinion. When I was a fledgling, first introduced to Sandy and training her to do my bidding, she still offered me at least one feeding per day from the syringe of yummies in the manner Brenda taught her. It was a bit undignified because it was messy, but it was tasty good, so I didn't complain.

It was also nice to have my new human dote on me in this way. There is a proper way to feed a baby bird, and that is to let his bird mom and bird dad do it. If the bird mom and bird dad appear to be screwing it up or if something's not working right, the human caregiver must step in to help, of course. You can't let a darling parrot like myself starve!

In the avian world, lots of humans argue, fuss, and fight over how to feed a young parrot. Let me tell you something. We parrots have fabulous tongues. There's a special hole in the back of the tongue that will close when we pump our necks to feed. Get the syringe in the beak and we'll do the rest. A wise African grey breeder named Jean Pattison wrote an article for Sandy's magazine all about this. You can read the article online with the pictures and everything.

Once you've grown past the fledgling stage, you'll want to eat more than baby formula, of course. We parrots cannot survive on formula all our lives. Our wild cousins out in the world must scrounge and forage for their foods; they spend a great part of the day looking for food sources. We are fortunate that our owners bring the food to us. Unfortunately, not all humans know what food is best for us. Let me tell you, if your human offers you a dish full of seeds, seeds, and more seeds, let out a CFS, dump over your dish, and poop on it from a high perch. If you give in to the temptation of eating a diet high in nasty seeds, you'll get too fat to move and your liver will fail. Don't do it.

Instead, train your human to give you a well-rounded diet of good foods. If your owner is not a trained nutritionist with a degree in chemical and molecular food science, then she will need to provide you with a formulated, pelleted diet from a company that employs a nutritionist. My human is not a nutritionist, but she is a journalist, so she knows how to research stuff. Sandy researched my diet and came up with this for each morning:

- One dish of non-colored pellets;
- One tablespoon of chopped veggie mashup;
- One to two nutri-berries or treats; and
- An almond or pistachio.

The avian veterinarian who performs my baseline bloodwork each year approves of the diet Sandy provides me, even if I am a few grams heftier than other sun conures. My liver and kidney function numbers always come back great; my digestive system and internal organs are fabulous. I'm an awesome bird overall, and I guess I can give her a little credit for the internal workings, although I'm smart enough not to eat all seeds.

Chopped Veggie Mashup Explained
While a formulated pelleted diet should make up sixty to seventy-five percent of a gorgeous parrot's daily diet, many owners have found value in offering a fresh vegetable mix as another twenty-five to thirty percent of the diet. The mashup is a *method* more than a recipe for getting lots of fresh foods into birds, but it's not a replacement for the researched and developed diets available from food manufacturers.

Several decades ago, before I was hatched, the concept of chopping up batches of vegetables and grains together to freeze in daily portions made feeding time more efficient for members of the avian breeding community. Owners back then didn't have multiple food vendors offering formulated pellets in the marketplace, but the smart ones knew better than to give handfuls of fattening seed to their special birds. Breeders who had large aviaries developed a complex recipe with optimized amounts of specific ingredients to ensure juvenile and adult birds took in proper nutrition.

Over the years, hobbyists and everyday pet bird owners have adapted the concept of chopping up batches of vegetables and grains to accommodate busy work schedules and limited offerings at the corner grocery store's produce department. By making changes to the original recipe, these well-meaning humans have negated its optimized nutrition.

The "bastardized" form of Chop that we see on the Internet today, and even in this chapter, is not the original, best recipe. This watered down, suggested version of chopped veggie mashup from my kitchen doesn't fill all nutritional needs of every bird encountered in the pet trade. Instead, it offers a good supplement of fresh veggies and vitamins to augment a pelleted diet.

In this chapter, I'll give the basic list of ingredients Sandy uses for the chopped veggie mashup in our tree. Notice she leaves out spinach, which some owners like to include. Sandy has kept reptiles for decades and has a love-hate relationship with spinach and its ability to bind and block the absorption of the calcium it delivers.

The point of this method is to cut and chop up good, healthy ingredients so that they mix and blend together in a way that makes them difficult for birds' beaks to separate. Keep in mind, you can augment and refine the list below to suit your flock's needs.

For example, Winston's vet has recommended he get more iron in his diet, so Sandy has a version of this recipe that includes additional quinoa, cooked amaranth, dried thyme, hearts of palm, and sprouted chickpeas. His version gets sprinkled with a pinch of moringa powder before it's served to him.

Cook quinoa, lentils, spelt, and pearled barley prior to adding them to the mix. Sandy doesn't cook the lentils completely; she doesn't let them get mushy.

For the pumpkin seeds, she puts a cup of them through the food processor with a cup of sliced almonds to make an almost sandy consistency to add to the mix. You may not want to have that much "fat" in your mix.

When your human has a version of this list, she should go over it with your avian vet to see what he/she would add or subtract for your species or your specific health needs. Make sure your vet knows you'll only receive this healthy mix as a portion of your diet. Your human won't replace what a degreed nutritionist has designed; she'll augment a proven diet with these fresh foods.

To make this chopped veggie mashup, Sandy learned from folks in the avian community to dry the ingredients as much as possible before adding them to the mix. The reason behind this is quality control. The method behind the madness is having ready-to-serve food each day without spending thirty to sixty minutes chopping up the ingredients every morning. By making a large batch of this mix and freezing it in daily portions, you make each day's feeding for the next couple of weeks easier to manage. But that management is lost if you thaw the mix into a soupy, goopy mess of gross vegetable stew. You want the ingredients to retain much of their structure.

Keep in mind, some folks in the avian community believe that freezing the daily portions in containers or baggies may destroy a small percentage of the foods' nutritional value. If that bothers your owner, then he can chop up enough food for a few days every three days until he gets overwhelmed by that schedule. Then he can try out prepping a month's worth at a time to see how that schedule works and still get healthy foods into you on a regular basis. It's a balancing act sometimes, but Sandy thinks getting ninety percent of a vegetable's nutrition into me is better than getting zero percent into me because of a time crunch.

Make sure your human removes the uneaten chopped veggie mashup after an hour or two so you don't have gross stuff in your cage attracting bacteria, fungus, and mold. If she forgets to take out a dish that starts to get warm, dump it over and poop on it from a high perch.

Here's the basic recipe that Sandy recommends, with some notes.

Sandy is careful with the **seeds**, adding two or three types per batch of mix.
- Pumpkin
- Sesame
- Flax
- Hulled hemp seed hearts
- Chia
- Millet
- Safflower

Make sure you give cooked **grains** time to drain and cool before adding them to the mix.
- Quinoa (tri-color is great)
- Oats (rolled, steel-cut)
- Oat groats
- Spelt
- Barley
- Lentils—red, split green peas
- Unsweetened coconut flakes
- Cayenne pepper flakes, crushed red pepper
- Kamut spiral pasta (high in protein)
- Veggie organic pasta

Vegetables/greens
- Ginger—helps upset tummies
- Turmeric—helps arthritic joints
- Golden beets
- Red beets
- Italian parsley—good calcium
- Carrots—good vitamin A
- English peas
- Parsnips

- Sweet potatoes—good vitamin A
- Different squashes
- Bok choy
- Turnip leaves, turnips
- Celery root
- Rutabaga
- Watercress—good calcium
- Rabbini—good calcium
- Broccoli rabe—good calcium
- Flowering/purple kale
- Kale
- Collard greens
- Mustard greens
- Red cabbage
- Raddiccio

Special Treats
From Petri's Kitchen
Remember that treats and homemade food items, while fully awesome, can't take the place of a nutritionist's formulated food. The researchers who develop pelleted and formulated diets for different sizes and species of birds do so with avian body weights and types in mind. Nutritional content-to-bodyweight ratios get worked out in a lab, not in the average human's kitchen.

Your owner needs to be cautious when making recipes that call for vitamin-rich, calcium-rich, or protein-rich ingredients, and then she can offer the resulting treats in small, tantalizing portions. Use your best judgment when accepting such treats from your human and use the experience to strengthen your relationship.

Here are a few of my favorite recipes with "room" for your human to make some notes to customize things to your beakie specifications.

Petri's Favorite Frilly Fruits
- ½ bunch frilly purple kale
- ½ cup diced lychees
- ½ cup diced raspberries
- 1 tablespoon hulled millet

Your human should:
Wash the kale and raspberries thoroughly. Peel and dice the lychees, throwing away the pit and red peel. You only want to use the white, fleshy fruit. Dice the raspberries. Tear up the kale into small, frilly chunks. Toss these in a bowl with the millet until everything is mixed. Spoon about a tablespoonfull of the mixture onto the side of the breakfast dish or on a treat dish. Remove uneaten portions about an hour to ninety minutes after serving. Remember, fruits attract bacteria, fungus, gnats, and all manner of problems to the cage. Don't leave fruit to ferment for hours on end.

Also, be aware of your bird's fruit intake. Certain birds—like lorikeets or toucans—*require* fruits and the sugars/complex carbohydrates they contain. Other parrots do not. Visit with your avian veterinarian about this before offering too much fruit. This special treat is just that: a treat.

Your Notes:

The Flock's Pumpkincicles
- 15-ounce can organic pureed pumpkin
- 1 cup non-dairy yogurt
- 1 teaspoon Ceylon cinnamon

Your human should:
Mix all three ingredients in a bowl. Scoop the mixture into at least two ice cube trays. Freeze. Serve to birdies.

With an approximate cost of $4.39 for this recipe, the twenty-four snacks come to about eighteen cents each. You can also add slivers of almonds or unsweetened coconut to give these treats more texture. You can also stick foot toys in these before freezing them to give them "handles" for bigger birds.

(Notice that this recipe specifies the use of Ceylon cinnamon. This spice is also available in Cassia cinnamon, which has been shown to thin blood. For best bird health, avian professionals recommend Ceylon cinnamon instead.)

Your Notes:

Parrot Summer Rolls
- 2 or 3 washed, full collard green leaves
- ½ cup peanut-free almond butter
- 3 tablespoons coconut oil
- ½ cup crushed walnuts
- ½ cup finely chopped broccoli rabe
- 1 finely chopped jalapeno pepper
- 1 tablespoon red cayenne pepper flakes
- Additional tablespoon of almond butter

Your human should:
Wash and pat dry the large, collard green leaves. Then set them aside on wax paper or a paper towel, etc. Chop the broccoli rabe and jalapeno pepper, mixing them together. (If your flock needs extra Vitamin A and C, go ahead and add some red or yellow bell pepper as well.) Mix the almond butter and coconut oil together until creamy smooth.

Spread the almond-butter-oil mix in a thin layer on each collard green leaf as if you're buttering a piece of bread. Evenly sprinkle the chopped veggies, then the chopped walnuts, and then the cayenne pepper flakes over the almond-butter-oil layer on each collard green leaf. Roll up each leaf. A dab of the extra almond butter can help "glue" the roll shut or use a bamboo cocktail stick that your bird can tear apart later.

Depending on bird size, you may wish to cut the roll into thirds before offering.

Your notes:

I hope the information I've presented in this book will help you pick the good foods from what your owner offers you. And I hope the information will help you teach and train your human to provide you the affection, attention, and excellent home we magnificent parrots deserve.

The first chapter includes some online resources as well to encourage your owner's continued education but remember to seek real-world advice from avian professionals. Sandy put together an online course (listed in the first chapter's resources) with some simple basics for your human. Pair that with this overall guide for training your human to do your bidding and you should have a wonderful bird life.

Epilogue

Preparing Your Human for the Rainbow Bridge
As a parrot—or any other type of bird—you play a vital role in caring for your owner. Depending on the species of bird you are, you should live with your human for the rest of his or her life. That's the goal. You should stay with the human you're responsible for and the human who is responsible for you should stay with you. The two of you make a commitment to care for one another when you become companions.

Sandy and I stayed together through everything. When she needed to move half-way across a continent, I had to travel in an obnoxious travel cage, but I moved with her. When she needed to get out of a crazy situation with a stinky boyfriend, I moved to a tiny apartment with her. I trained her and cared for her always.

Just as your human will be watching out for your best health, it's up to you to watch for changes in his or her health. For example, Sandy started to have issues with kidney stones a long time ago, and I knew the stones were about to cause her a problem. I walked down her back and tugged on her waist band as close to her kidney as I could get. I muttered about the problem, so she'd know what was about to happen. Even though she was easy to train, she didn't catch on to what I was trying to tell her until after she ended up in the emergency room with the awful kidney stone pain.

A couple of years after that, when Sandy had health issues, I was just figuring out that it was pretty cool to snuggle against her neck to stay warm. I noticed she had illness sneaking into her body. I would lie against her chest where I could sense some tumors were growing and I would mutter and squeak about the problem until she finally went to the doctor. Thank goodness the doctors took care of that so she could be my human mom for all my life.

To keep your person flight ready, you'll want to preen him or her on a regular basis. You never know when you'll be called home to Heaven and your human will have to do these things on her own.

One of the worst things your human will experience is your passing from this world to the next. For most of us birds, we'll outlive our owners for a few reasons.

One of the reasons is some people don't realize they want to have an intelligent and fabulous companion to share their lives with until they are older in years. When a person who is sixty or more years old realizes he needs a feathered companion in life, he might purchase or adopt a young bird who will live more years than he has left to live. This is a sad thing for the bird, of course. The human you train and love will someday pass away, leaving you to find a new person to train—and hopefully come to love—until it's your time to pass on and find peace in Heaven.

Another reason we outlive our owners is the fact we parrots live a long time. Some of us are predisposed to live up to eighty years. Some of us, like the magnificent species of conures, may only live for twenty or thirty years. Prepare yourself for this next statement.

I only lived with Sandy for nineteen years.

The night before I had a stroke, I let Sandy know I wanted to sit with her on the couch. It was a Friday night and she was happy to sit with me and let me cuddle against her neck. I made sure her hair was preened and that she was flight ready. I even let her take a couple pictures of us with the evil camera. Something in me told me it would be important to her later.

When it was my time to pass Saturday morning, Sandy went with me to the vet clinic and cuddled me all the way there. She held me and comforted me, like a good owner should. I'm not sure that she was completely ready for that morning, so I might not be the right bird to share *how* to prepare your human for this emotionally devastating moment. But when the moment comes, a well-trained human will step up to care for you as best as he or she can.

Your person will offer you the sweetest kisses and kindest words. When the moment comes, I hope you won't have any need to be afraid. Your owner will do anything and everything she can to comfort you and make sure you have every soft and pleasant thing.

Because you've trained her right and built a wonderful relationship, your human will make sure you have no more pain, no more worry, and nothing to fret about at all.

About the Authors

Petri is a sun conure with a high level of patience with his human. He taught Sandy the meaning of unconditional love.

Sandy Lender is a magazine editor by day and author of girl-power fantasy novels by night. You can check out her author page on Amazon or follow her facebook page at Fantasy Author Sandy Lender. She lives in Florida where she volunteers in sea turtle conservation and parrot rescue. She gave a presentation at the American Federation of Aviculture in 2018 and published an avian magazine for six years while working fulltime as the editor of an international construction magazine. She has two APEX Awards in technical writing and a 2019 IMADJINN Award for Best Literary Fiction Novel. Visit her website at www.SandyLenderInk.com.

Other Works by Sandy Lender include a number of short stories in juried anthologies and…

The *Choices* Series

Choices Meant for Gods, ArcheBooks Publishing, 2007

Choices Meant for Kings, ArcheBooks Publishing, 2009

Choices Meant for All, ArcheBooks Publishing, 2015

What Choices We Made, Vol 1, 2008

What Choices We Made, Vol 2, 2010

The *Dragons in Space* Series

Problems on Eldora Prime

Problems Above Pangaea Moon

May Your Heart be Light

We Can't Let You In

She's Not Broken

How to Train Your Human: A Guide for Parrots

CPSIA information can be obtained
at www.ICGtesting.com
Printed in the USA
BVHW031449131220
595622BV00009B/127